MW00904673

CLIMATE AND WEATHER

BOOKS FOR KIDS

Children's Earth Sciences Books

BABY PROFESSOR

EDUCATION KIDS

Snow in the summer! Picnic weather in the middle of winter! Bigger storms than ever before! The Earth seems to be moving into a time of extreme weather. Read on and learn more!

A Tornado forming in the evening from a supercell.

WHAT IS "EXTREME WEATHER"?

Extreme weather is weather events happening when they aren't expected, where they aren't expected, and in a scale out of the ordinary. If it rains a lot on a desert where it has hardly ever rained in the past fifty years, that's extreme weather. If the sky dumps a month's supply of rain on a city in six hours, that's extreme weather.

However, major weather events are not called "extreme", even if they are very powerful, if they happen regularly in that part of the world at that season of the year. For example, Oklahoma has "tornado alley", where huge, destructive wind funnels appear regularly. They are important and dangerous events, but because they are a regular feature on that part of the Earth, they don't count as "extreme weather".

Huge hurricane approaching Florida in America. Elements of this image furnished by NASA.

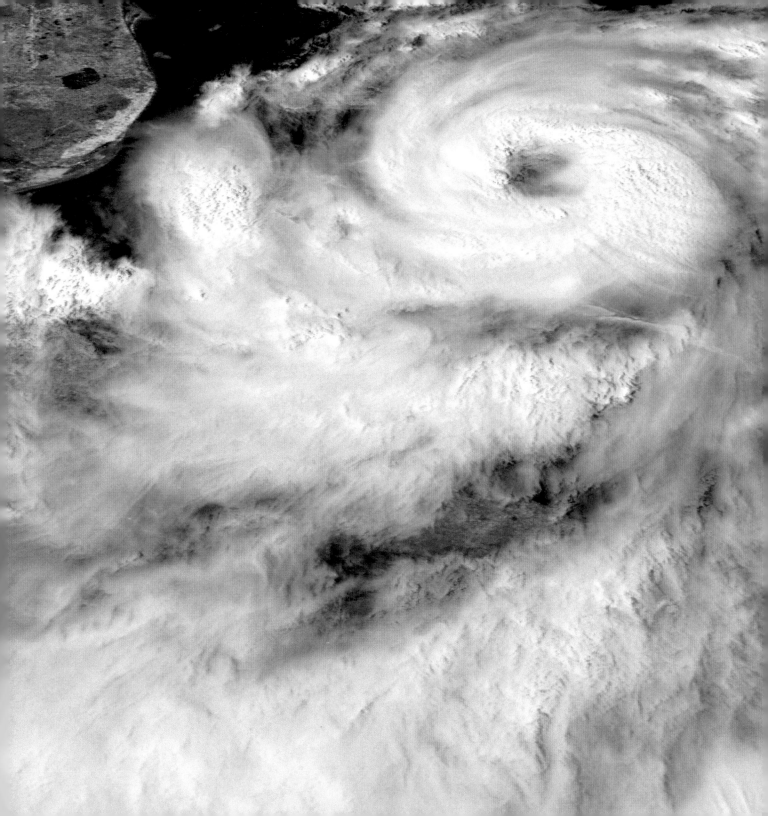

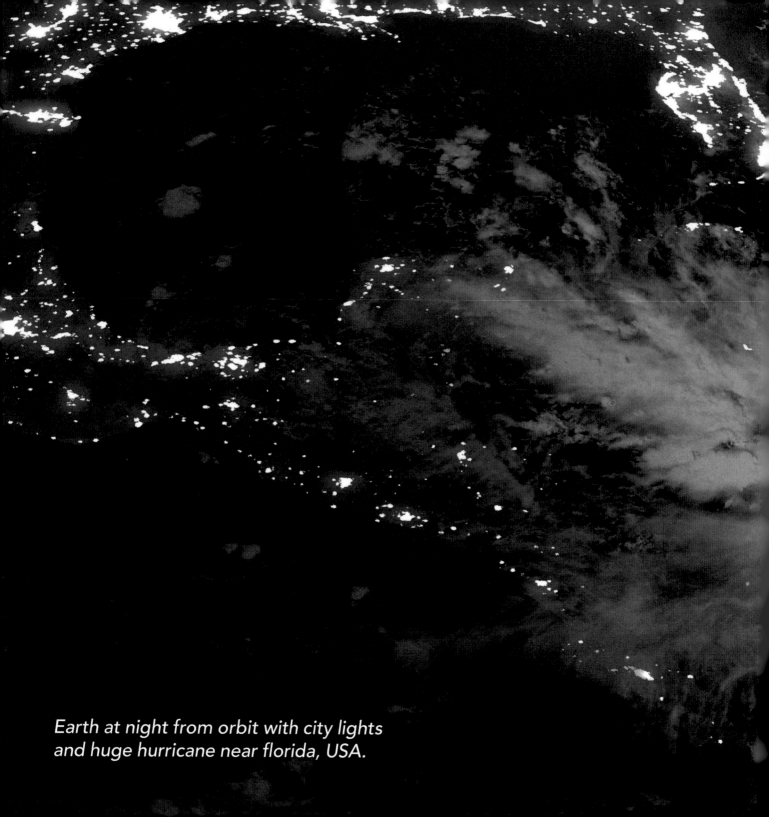

Earth at night from orbit with city lights and huge hurricane near florida, USA.

Meteorologists and weather forecasters keep and study careful records of what the weather tends to do at the same time each year. Farmers rely on such knowledge: they know that April will be rainy where they live, but May is usually drier and warmer, so they plan to plant their crops in May.

Cruise-ship operators know that, traditionally, hurricanes rip through the Caribbean at a certain time of year, so they send their ships to visit other places during those months.

For forecasters, extreme weather is events that lie in the most unusual 10% of recorded weather—weather that is wetter, or drier, or windier, or whatever than all but 10% of the days for that time of year for that place on the planet.

When the weather catches us by surprise, it can cause damage to property, destroy animal and fish habitats, and cause many deaths.

Clouds seen from airplane.

El Niño Conditions

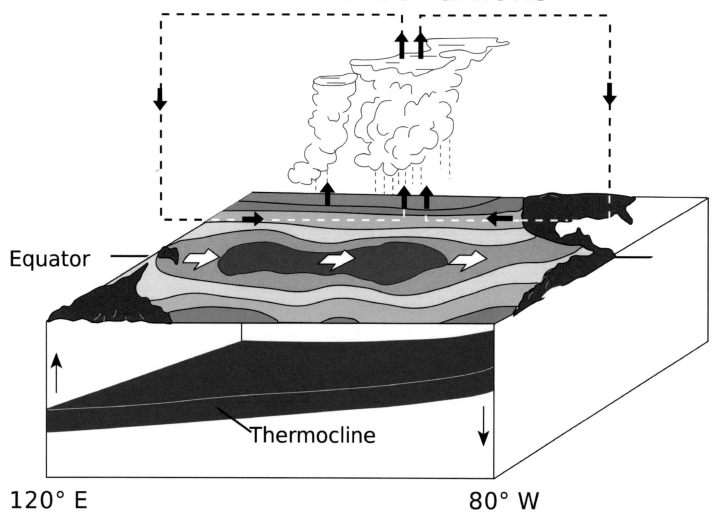

Equator

Thermocline

120° E

80° W

WHAT CAUSES EXTREME WEATHER?

Scientists say that the Earth has gotten dramatically warmer over the past hundred years. This global warming has changed air currents, water currents, the behavior of clouds.

Weather patterns can have far-felt effects. For example, there are two big currents in the Pacific Ocean, El Niño (Warm Water) and La Niña (Colder Water). How those currents move affects rainfall patterns right across North America, possibly causing unusually dry or wet years.

La Niña Conditions

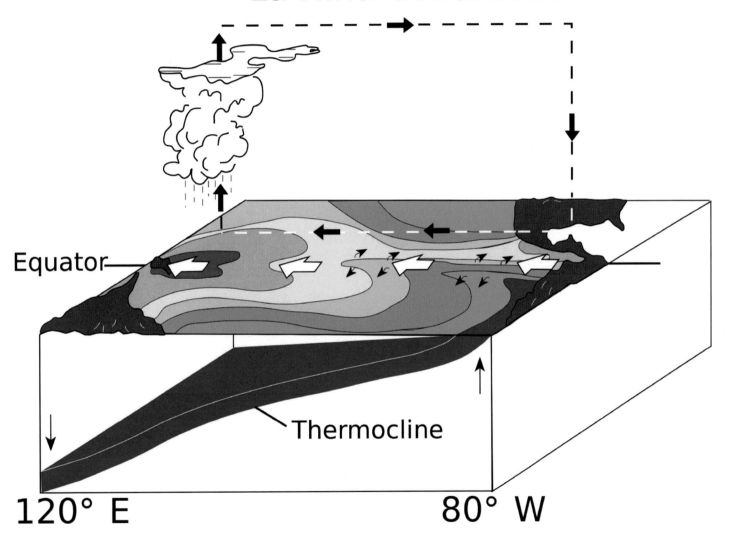

Equator

Thermocline

120° E   80° W

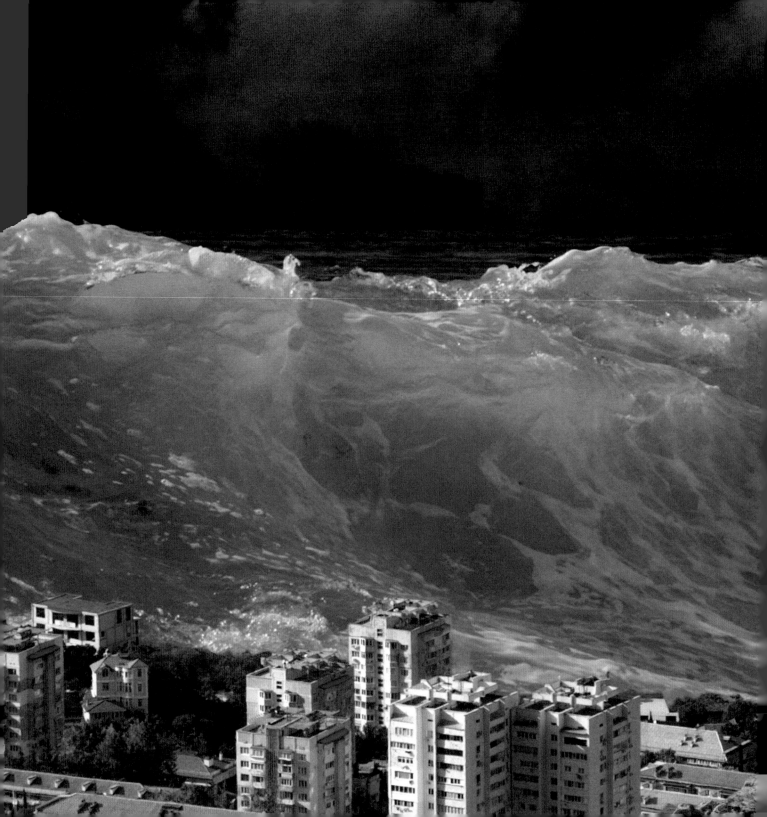

There are other causes of extreme weather events. For instance, an undersea earthquake can cause a huge tsunami, a wall of water many feet tall that can crash into the nearest coast, destroying buildings and knocking down trees for a long distance inland.

Giant tsunami waves crashing small coastal town.

A sun flare.

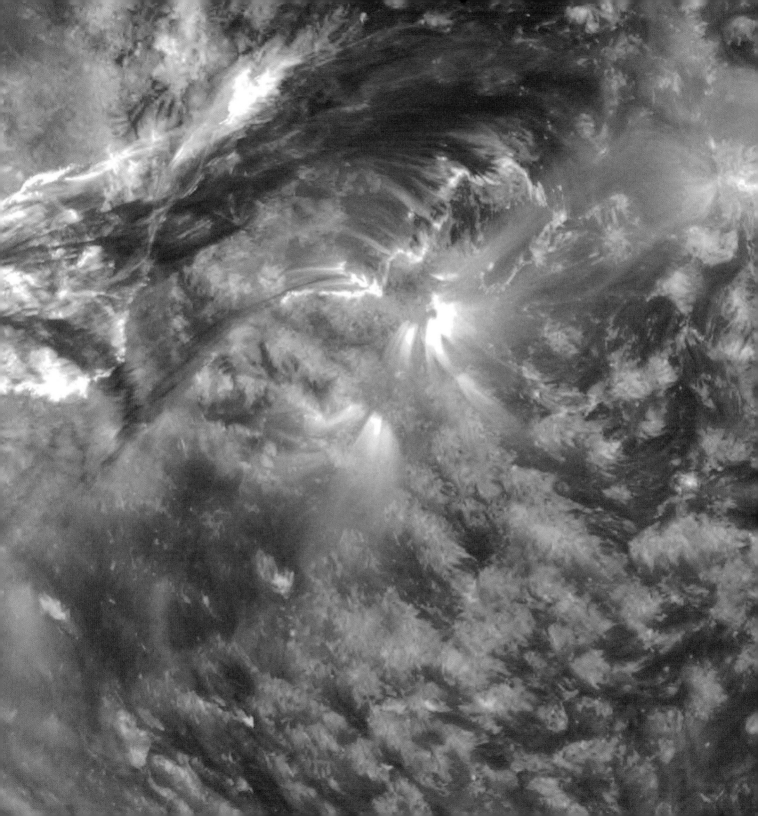

EXTREME WEATHER AROUND THE WORLD

HEAT WAVES

India, Australia, and other countries have been suffering through very high temperatures in their already-hot summers. Temperatures have risen to over 120 degrees Fahrenheit in cities, and have stayed at that level for days, causing thousands of deaths of both people and animals. Poor people, who have no access to air conditioning and don't have the option to travel to a cooler part of the world for a while, suffer and die. Cattle herds suffer both from the heat and from the lack of water.

Summer temperatures throughout Europe have not risen so high, but they have broken all previous records in Paris and other cities. Fewer people in Europe have died directly from the heat, but all people in the area have been suffering.

Exhausting summer heat in the Park.

Forest fire danger.

FOREST FIRES

Fires are a normal part of the lifecycle of wild forests. However, the fire season has been starting earlier, lasting longer, and covering more acres in recent years in the Pacific Northwest of the United States and Canada.

A combination of high temperatures, unusually strong winds, and dry conditions caused by an extended drought are letting fires spread and grow far beyond normal. Smoke from these fires affects the atmosphere as far east as Minnesota.

ICE MELTING

Greenland's ice sheet is the largest mass of ice outside of Antarctica. It is retreating far further in warm weather than ever before in recorded history. The disappearance of the ice not only adds waters to the ocean, raising the ocean levels; there is an increase in earthquake activity throughout Greenland as the disappearance of masses of ice makes the ground unstable.

Icebergs in the Antarctic.

COLD WAVES

While the general effect of global warming is to warm the whole Earth, changes in weather patterns mean that sometimes there will be sudden cold snaps, snow far later in the year than is normal, or storms of hail and sleet. These weather events can attack young crops as they are getting established, destroying harvests over wide areas.

Early 2012 European cold wave in Sarajevo.

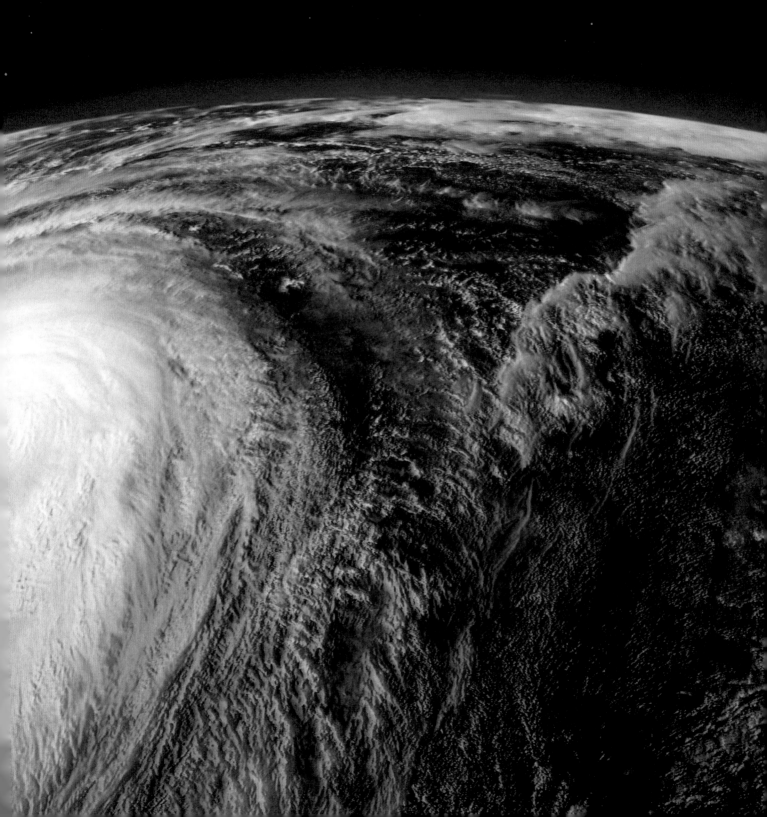

HURRICANE SEASON

"Hurricane Season" in the Caribbean and Central America traditionally runs from June to the end of November, with the most hurricanes developing and threatening the land between the middle of August and the middle of September.

However, in recent years hurricane season has been getting longer, with larger and more powerful storms developing sooner and having a wider impact. These new storms at unexpected times are extreme weather, for they are not happening when all our records and experience expect them to.

RAINFALL

December, 2015 was the wettest month in England since records started being kept, with twice the normal amount of rain and snow falling. This lead to flooding of roads and whole towns in the north of England.

Summer storm.

Hurricane Sandy

CASCADING EVENTS

One of the challenges of extreme weather is that it is just not one thing. A huge storm not only brings a lot of rain; it brings high winds that can knock over power lines, damage buildings, and make flooding worse. If this happens in an area that has experienced an extended drought (a different extreme weather event), the ground is unable to absorb the water appropriately. Flash floods and mud slides can happen, carrying away dams, roads and bridges.

An unusually large and powerful storm may bring with it lightning that starts fires or knocks out parts of the electrical grid.

If the storm has knocked out power, it may mean that the supply of fresh water is reduced because pumping stations are offline. Water-treatment stations may flood, sending untreated sewage into streets and lawns.

New York after Hurricane Sandy

If flooding and high winds have damaged roads and bridges, it may be hard for emergency vehicles to get through if a fire starts or a building collapses. People may be stuck in traffic jams far from home, unable to leave their cars and unable to get anywhere dry and safe. People who need to get to hospitals, or even to get food and supplies, cannot easily get where they need to go.

Flooded street.

Then the challenge for the community is: what do you fix first? Nations and local authorities try to develop plans for dealing with emergencies, but an extreme weather event can outrun even the best response plan.

Flooded city of Wroclaw in 2010.

Communities and scientists are starting to look at what extreme weather events might bring to local areas in the coming years. They want to put in place resources so communities can respond not just to a neighborhood, but a whole city, being flooded by a combination of heavy rain, high tide, and whipping winds.

Wreckage and debris from homes destroyed by devastating fire during Hurricane Sandy. 111 homes were destroyed in the out-of-control blaze.

Insurance companies are part of the effort to improve preparations. Insurance claims for storm damage across all of Canada used to average about $800 million a year in the 1980s. In 2013 a combination of extreme-weather events sent claims up to $3.2 billion.

Since projections indicate that extreme weather events will get more frequent, damage, and therefore the cost of fixing things after a storm or flood, is likely to continue to increase.

Halifax, Nova Scotia, for example, is a seaport city. It is used to heavy, wet storms in both summer and winter. But those storms are becoming more frequent and more fierce. A study projected that the Halifax area may see annual damage from storms in the region of $20 million dollars by the year 2030.

But the report also showed that just one super-storm, the sort of event that used to be called a "Century Storm" because it was supposed to show up only about once in a hundred years, could cause over $100 million in damage. And extreme weather events, including super-storms, are becoming more and more frequent.

On the west coast of North America, there is an effort to make sure that schools can withstand a flood and provide safe refuge for students and the community. A major event like an earthquake in the Pacific Ocean could send a tsunami, a wave higher than most buildings, toward the coastline of North America with little warning.

Cracked asphalt road.

The new effort is to strengthen school buildings so that everyone could take shelter in the upper floors while flood waters fill the lower floor, in confidence that the building would not fall down under the stress of the extreme weather event.

COMING WEATHER EVENTS

What may we look for in the way of weather in months and years to come? We seem to be moving into an unsettled period when extreme weather events may become the "new normal". Read Baby Professor books like *What Every Child Should Know about Climate Change* to learn more.

Made in the USA
Monee, IL
20 November 2020

By the end of the afternoon, I was beginning to get tired because we had been at the competition all day. Finally, my last match was called up and it was for the bronze medal!

I had never won a medal before, and I started to picture myself smiling on the podium with a huge bronze medal. What would my friends at school say if I came to school on Monday with a big, shiny medal?

I walked out for my third and final fight, my heart was beating through my chest, my palms were sticky, and my arms and legs felt numb. My opponent and I gripped up and we both attacked and defended with ferocity, trying to throw each other with various trips and takedown attempts.

After three minutes of fighting there was still no takedown. We were still on our feet pushing and pulling trying to gain the upper hand. Finally, after what felt like ten minutes, my opponent took me down with an inside trip and within a few seconds I managed to sweep him and get on top landing inside my opponents legs. In BJJ we call this position closed guard.

Now the score was 2-2 but I needed to get into a better position in order to gain a submission victory.

As the fight continued my legs and arms began to weaken. It felt like I had no energy left in them. My forearms and shoulders were screaming in pain as I fought to stop my opponent getting a better position on me. I began to want to quit the match. I wanted to give up. I wanted to let my opponent beat me so I could have a rest from the fight. A bronze medal is cool, but I didn't think it was worth the extra effort needed to win it.

Mid way through the match I looked over and saw my Mum excitedly cheering me on. Then I saw my Professor and I remembered what he told me after I lost my second match. He told me that he wanted to see me try my best. To leave it all out on the mat. Quitting was not giving it my absolute best. I decided that I had to try and give it my all, no matter whether I won or lost. So I grit my teeth, took a deep breath and tried to get to a better position.

But, my opponent read my movements and counter attacked me with a triangle choke. I tried to fight my way out of it but the submission was on too tight. All I could do was tap out and accept defeat as my opponent celebrated the win, claiming the bronze medal and leaving me in a tired heap on the floor.

I was so worn out after the match; I could barely walk off the mat. I cried in front of everyone and was so sad. However, I was met by high fives, hugs and smiles as my coach and teammates told me how well I did. Some people even said it was the match of the day!

That night I went to bed exhausted, but so happy. I couldn't believe that I had competed in a BJJ competition. I was proud of myself. I had overcome all my fears and faced the competition courageously. It didn't matter that I lost in front of all those people, because they only cheered me on and said how strong I had been to take up the challenge. I felt like I could do anything!

The following day, I was sore all over my body. Who would have thought that a few grappling matches could leave you so tired and sore? My entire body ached in places I had never felt before.

I usually walk to school, but I was so exhausted from the tournament the day before that Mum dropped me off for class.

During History class, the teacher said that our next assignment would be a presentation. I felt the familiar sick feeling in my stomach that usually goes with public speaking.

However, this time I had a tool to use. I closed my eyes, took a couple of deep breaths and accessed my inner strength. As my thoughts became clearer, I remembered back to the competition, when I didn't quit and tried my very best. I realized that if I can handle the pressures of competing in a BJJ competition, then I could do absolutely anything!

I sat back in my chair and smiled. I couldn't wait for my next BJJ competition.

Matthew D'Aquino is a Judo Olympian and author from Canberra, Australia. He has represented Australia at eight Continental Championships, four World Championships and competed in the 2008 Beijing Olympic Games. He is also a BJJ Black Belt under Felipe Grez.

Matt is passionate about all things Judo and Brazilian Jiujitsu and has helped thousands of grapplers worldwide through his online resources, eBooks and online content which can be found at beyondgrappling.com and the Universityofjudo.com

CPSIA information can be obtained
at www.ICGtesting.com
Printed in the USA
LVHW020921171220
674418LV00005B/370